Introduction/About the book

This data isn't introduced by a clinical expert and is for instructive and educational purposes as it were. The substance isn't planned to sub for proficient clinical exhortation,

 finding, or treatment .

Continuously look for the exhortation of your doctor or other qualified medical services supplier with any inquiries you might have in regards to an ailment. Never dismiss proficient clinical exhortation or defer in looking for it due to something you have perused or heard.

About the author

I'm Dealer Blunt the eldest son of Jimmy

Author's, media personality and activist.

The Believing Church is in trouble, so I fasted to build a television ministry.

I'm not referring to the current socio-political animosity that is erasing Christianity and even making it into a pariah. I'm talking about a more internal situation.

As a Christian, you have been given authority by God; therefore, free yourself to utilize it.

Putting God foremost

FIND THE BETTER SELF SECRET; AND DISCOVER A SECRET TO A STRESS-FREE LIFE

Dealer Blunt

TABLE OF CONTENTS

Chapter: 1

HOW Inspiration Increments Confidence

With regards to inspiration, you will see that it accomplishes more than getting you rolling. It gets you to the place where you can be and connect to acknowledge the things the way they are. There are so many ways that one would agree that it can increase self esteem. There are such countless justifications for why you attempt to find something that propels you so you can in the end be more joyful with what your identity is and with your life. The main way to cap inspiration will expand your confidence is for the way that it will take a gander at the status quo. With inspiration you will find there are times when you will actually want to take a gander at your existence with a reasonable head and afterward have the option to choose what and where you might want to go from that point. The second way that inspiration will expand your confidence is for the way that once things begin to turn out for you, you will feel better about yourself. You will see an adjustment of your disposition about existence and you'll really have the option to appreciate life. You will simply rest easier thinking about yourself since you will see the chance for change that you have.

You will actually want to see the value in the way that you can get things done and you will feel more anxious to put yourself out there and reach for far superior things. The third way that inspiration will build your confidence is that it will give you boldness. From the achievement that you will find from your self inspiration you will actually want to drive yourself to go for other

things that you might not have pondered and you'll likewise drive yourself to contemplate everything that you should investigate. Things that you should seek after from here on out. This is an extraordinary approach to living since you can start to find the slight gs that really fulfill you. Since you will You will feel like a triumph and find success in your very own accomplishments. Something else about inspiration is that it will make you see things in a positive light. At the point when things start to go perfectly and everything winds up the manner in which you plan it to be, you'll rest easier thinking about yourself and about everything in your life. You will start to meaningfully impact the manner in which you think from a negative light to a positive light. All that will appear to change since you are thinking in an unexpected way.

At the point when you start to think positively you value the more modest things throughout everyday life. can regard others and to Inspiration is vital on the grounds that you will not have the option to prevail with regards to anything that you wish until you can drive yourself. You want motivation in your life so you have motivation to accomplish more with your life. It makes you need to change into a superior individual.

Without inspiration there are a great deal of things in life that would appear to be pointless. Inspiration helps you have an improved outlook on your mythical person since you will turn out to be brimming with confidence. At the point when you are propelled to follow through with something, there is an incredible sense that you can accomplish these things. That makes it worth doing; knowing and accepting that you are completely equipped for accomplishing something that y ou really want. Inspiration is an extraordinary inclination; nonetheless, you simply have to find the proper thing to get you rolling. You should simply find something that you can be energetic about. Inspiration will expand your self awareness.esteem and sell

Chapter: 2

HOW Inspiration WILL Build YOUR Efficiency AT WORK

Self Motivation is extremely difficult to create, notwithstanding, assuming you have something in your life that you are capable and ready to buckle down for, you ought to have the option to spur yourself to pull out all the stops. Inspiration will expand your work efficiency; nonetheless, you want to have motivating obligations for your work. The thing with a great many people is that they simply don't have some work that they believe is significant. They don't play a part in the work environment that makes them feel satisfied. You will need to ensure that you secure something in the positions that you take so you can be enlivened and roused to go all the way with the gig. The way to ensure that you work is persuasive is searching for ways that you might have expected in the gig. These ways could imply that you can predict an advancement or start a new position with the commitment of a raise. You will need to ensure that you take some work that will give you space to develop so you have something to hold back nothing. You will need to ensure additionally that you can invest the energy and work into the task to cause it to appear satisfying. This means that in the event that you realize that you will be taking some work that calls for a great deal of your investment and consideration, then, at that point, you should be prepared to give it.

On the off chance that you wind up taking some work that is beyond what you can deal with you won't be spurred to say the least. Let's say that you have the potential, yet you simply don't have the energy to invest the energy. How would it be advisable for you to respond? The main thing that you will believe should do is wonder why you don't feel the energy to produce your own self inspiration, there should be something that is keeping you down. It is possible that you are frightened to have the additional obligations. You may simply be stressed over the way others see you. More often than not, when you are not inspiring yourself it is on the grounds that you have a close to home or mental clash of some sort. You may only not be prepared for more work, but rather you want to continue on. You should simply move past all o f your work weaknesses and put stock in yourself. The most un-that you will at any point need to do is have confidence in yourself. In the event that you can accept that you can follow through with something, you will track down the inspiration to build your efficiency. There is a tremendous justification for why you should attempt to propel yourself. The main motivation why you want to find inspiration is so you can make something out of your life and profession. That doesn't imply that you need to go for President, notwithstanding, you will rest easier thinking about your accomplishments assuming you work for them, rather than simply getting them given to you. You will observe that the inspiration for your efficiency is significant in the numbers.

In the event that you work harder, others will as well, and the organization will see these little accomplishments and afterward give rewards for your persistent effort. laborers. The general purpose of expanding your efficiency is in order to be seen by upper administration or by getting a gesture of congratulations from a portion of your co. You really want to peer inside yourself and find a piece of your work or career that you like and afterward stay with it. You ought to likewise ensure that you generally acknowledge a task that will give you a promising future and something to anticipate.

The thing with the individuals who are attempting to recover from drugs is that you really want a specific measure of inspiration so you can remain clean and stay away from tumbling off the cart. Where does such inspiration remain inside an individual? A large portion of the inspiration that a recuperating fiend needs comes from inside to sew. For a recuperating fiend to remain clean they need to remain clean. There are such countless motivations behind why individuals attempt to remain clean, yet it is for the most part from the apprehension about losing the affection and solace that they have come acclimated with. Individuals tidy up so t hello can keep their agreeable lives. This is only one of the inspirations, but there are more motivations behind why you might need to get perfect and sober. What are the reasons that you are thinking about getting perfect for? There are so many, yet they all have a touch of inspiration within them that you can urge yourself to remain clean. Such countless individuals will tumble off the cart; be that as it may, in the event that you simply find the inspiration then you will actually want to recuperate from anything. Additionally, you really want to find the motivation to acknowledge reality.

This implies that you can't take cover behind the feeling of the medications. You can't goof and afterward return to self pity. The inspiration that you really want to find is the inspiration to acknowledge what your identity is and to track down the boldness to transform it. There are such countless individuals who figure out how to remain clean since they don't permit themselves to have sympathy. They are roused to get up and assume responsibility for their life. At the point when you are on drugs, you are not responsible for your life. The medications are in charge, yet with the legitimate measure of inspiration, you ought to have the option to own the difficult situations and return out of recovery with a decent, strong understanding of life and reality. With regards to finding inspiration, there are so many things that you can go to so you can track down the inspiration. You can go to your loved ones for the help that you really want to track down in yourself to get off the medications and remain off. You can likewise hurl yourself entirely into an action. You can figure out how to paint, draw, compose, play , whatever permits you to remove the concentration from your requirement for drugs. At the point when you go to these things rather than the medications you will find that things will get much simpler extra time. You will not have such countless desires and you'll be motivated. There are numerous artists that foster a secret ability as a result of their capacity to connect for life rather than drugs. The general purpose of finding your inspiration for your recovery is finding something that you can rest on until you can remain all alone. at the point when you get snared

On drugs you can go through years reliant upon your next fix, and it is difficult to rely upon yourself when you have been contingent upon substances for such a long time. That is the reason you want to find something that will persuade you to remain perfect and that you ca n use as a bolster. It doesn't need to be someone else, yet it very well may be. In the event that you can rest on a nearby relative or cherished one until you can remain all alone, you will find your inspiration from the relationship similar to a craftsman finding motivation in a work of art.

Chapter: 3

Inspiration TO Move AWAY FROM ADDICTIONS

It doesn't make any difference what your addictions are. The main thing that matters is that you will track down ways of defeating them. You really want to find the right inspiration before you anticipate stopping or you won't ever make it. As a matter of fact, in the event that you're not sufficiently able to recuperate a great many people will wind up tumbling off the cart and hitting their addictions harder than at any other time. You would rather not put yourself in peril. You simply have to unwind and find something inside of you that will give you the inspiration from returning to the addictions. You really want the inspiration that comes from inside yourself, as well as, the help of others for you to make it all alone, compulsion free. A large portion of the inspiration that you will find will come from inside yourself. In the event that you don't believe that you need to stop for yourself, then you won't ever stop. You need to ensure that this is the sort of thing that you need for yourself. You should ensure that it is something that you believe shouldn't be on the grounds that you feel constrained or compelled to do. In the event that you truly are focused on your restoration, you will start to track down more motivation to assist you with needing to recuperate. The initial step is hard, it's the expression "No". The subsequent step is much harder. The second step implies you need to say no for eternity.

Chapter: 4

Inspiration FOR Recuperating Medication Junkies

To find the limitations that you will require you should start to rest on your level-headed and clean companions or family and afterward additionally on things like artistic expression or exercises that you might become keen on. Then once you track down something that you can do rather than the addictions you will go more grounded and roused to make a perfect and sober life for yourself. Be that as it may, not every person generally dislikes remaining spotless and level-headed, a few addictions don't circumvent drugs. There are different things like sex, the web, and betting addictions that may be an issue. In these cases you will find strength in individuals around you and you might need to get a specialist to assist you with adapting to the desires and with the dependence. Motivat particle comes from such countless things and you will track down many items that help you from annihilating your life. There are such countless things that you really want to free yourself up to so you can track down inspiration to move away from the horrendous way of behaving. When you have stomach muscles to get an embrace of life and reality you might need to contemplate a portion of the things that inspire you to remain clean. Things like your companions, family, and side interests can be a major piece of your recuperation, yet you really want to figure out how to stick to what persuades you so you don't want to return to the betting or no matter what. When you find a smidgen of inspiration that keeps you from the compulsion, you will require more things.

Things that will give you the solidarity to remain clean and away from your habit-forming ways of behaving and the main way you can do this is assuming you figure out how to persuade yourself and to be affected by the positive reactions that everyone around you provide for you on the side of your recuperation. Support from companions and family is 'where' you will get the boldness and solidarity to proceed with your recuperation. You will require the help the most when you want to goof, yet by utilizing the inspiration that you get from others and from yourself you ought to be capable of recuperating with next to no slip outs.

Chapter: 5

The most effective method to Spur YOURSELF

With regards to spurring yourself you will observe that it is the hardest thing to do. It is simply such a ton more straightforward to express your feelings to others than it is to offer yourself some counsel. You may be the sort who can without much of a stretch be roused, yet you probably won't be, one way or the other, spurring yourself is still hard. The way to inspire yourself is to find a decent, strong confidence level. You really want to regard what your identity is and furthermore acknowledge yourself for what your identity is. You might have the option to talk your
sentiments out with somebody who is near you and they will assist with directing you, yet on the off chance that you just knew exactly the way in which extraordinary it feels to

spur yourself. Assuming that you might want to figure out how to assist with the way that you feel about yourself you might need to think
about looking for direction.

It's anything but terrible to see somebody about your sentiments, as a matter of fact, it very well may be a decent and strong approach to your absence of inspiration. When you can chip away at yourself, you will actually want to unblock every one of your channels
What's more, track down obvious inspiration to go for something. There are so many alternate ways that you can spur yourself. You will have
 to find the things that you truly view as intriguing. There are such countless individuals who simply come up short on motivation, yet once they find something that grabs their attention they are roused to go further after it.

That incorporates the antagonism that you might experience by not arriving at your point. Notwithstanding, in the event that you figure out how to track down the solidarity to continue to attempt you will track down the inspiration to keep your reach skyward. To persuade yourself is the hardest undertaking that you may at any point have, notwithstanding, it is totally worth the effort in the end when you achieve your objective realizing that you did it totally all alone. You will find that you can be totally cheerful realizing that you can do something all alone for yourself.

Chapter: 6

Instructions to Propel OTHERS

You might feel that it is not difficult to propel others, yet that relies upon their character, as well as yours. You may not be the kind of individual who can aim for somebody, in any case, you might only highlight a dear cherished one to find something that they really have an enthusiastic outlook on. However, you might need to ponder how you express things before you say it. At the point when you ponder how you are falling off to the next then you ought to be able to have the stuff to inspire somebody. With regards to the way that you make statements you must glance at how you are moving toward the subject, the manner of speaking that you are utilizing, as well as, the words that you use. With regards to correspondence individuals don't understand that it probably won't be what they are talking about, yet the way in which they are saying it. You need to ensure that you can impart your message properly. The principal thing that you need to do is take out the 'you' as would be natural for you. At the point when you use words like " I think You." you will observe that somebody will get on the guard. You will observe that others will misinterpret you and things will come out right. You will likewise need to take out every one of the negative remarks out of your persuasive discourse.

You can't persuade somebody by putting them down. You can't attempt to get somebody to move by pushing them. It simply doesn't work that way. You should watch the words that you utilize and the way that you say them so you can decidedly build up all that you might want to say and move the individual. Notwithstanding, for you to get the image of the individual that you are attempting to spur, you must learn how to tune in. Listening can be extremely hard when you are used to doing all the talking. Nonetheless, you will have to figure out how to or you will always be unable to speak with somebody completely. Before you proceed to attempt to converse with somebody about getting hey m or her to discover some inspiration you must wonder why the person in question genuinely should track down something. This is significant on the grounds that you would rather not mistake your thought processes in the circumstance. You want to persuade somebody since you need the best for the person in question, not due to what you need in your life. Rousing anyone is hard. You should simply ensure that you are there for the individual and that you are there for them when they need you. This is significant in light of the fact that your help will propel them to connect for far superior things. Assuming you can simply be a companion to the individual, you will find that in the end you will urge them to be a superior individual. There are so many ways to energize somebody.

You should simply show up for them as an emotionally supportive network and keep the correspondence lines open. You will likewise need to continue to propose groundbreaking thoughts so they might find something that persuades them. This is an extraordinary method for starting a more grounded and closer relationship with somebody and helping that person track down the correct way. Any individual who can be an old buddy can propel an individual to connect for far superior things. Any individual who can be an old buddy can inspire an individual to connect for greater and better things.

Chapter: 7

Inspiration AND Setting aside Cash.

You realize what persuades individuals to set aside cash. Dread. Dread assists individuals with getting into the saving propensity since it causes individuals to understand that they can lose everything. You will wind up losing numerous things on the off chance that you don't I bring in how to deal with your cash. Try not to hold on until something has occurred, such as getting your vehicle removed from you. You will need to ensure that you need to track down the inspiration right off the bat throughout everyday life. In the event that you figure out how to set aside your cash a smidgen at a time you may have the option to have a decent hunk of progress eventually. Setting aside cash is significant on the grounds that no one can really tell when the difficult situations will hit. You will observe that there is a great deal of inspiration in realizing that you can have a wellbeing. With regards to a security net, you will find that it has a tremendous open door since no one can really tell what will occur. Setting aside cash is vital in light of the fact that no one can tell what could occur. You might wind up losing your employment. You might wind up getting injured. You want to ensure that you can cover yourself by setting aside the cash.

A few different things that could come into mind when you are searching for inspiration for setting aside cash is something that you generally cared about. Perhaps you have a reason to set aside the cash and it isn't for a rainy day. Perhaps you need to set aside your cash so you can disappear on holiday, buy a vehicle, buy a home, buy something gigantic that you regularly wouldn't buy. You will contemplate how much cash it will take to make the pursuit and afterward you must buckle down setting aside the cash. This is an obvious motivation to set aside some cash since you will cherish yourself eventually. You will understand what it seems like to buckle down for something that you really care about. On the off chance that setting aside cash for something specific isn't what you believe you should do then you should set aside the cash for your future. There are such countless individuals who are from the child blasting age who are currently stressed over how they will make it. They are stressed over how they are going to have the option to live after retirement. It's terrifying to be at an age where you can't work and not have any cash to put something aside for what's to come. To be roused to set aside cash then you ought to constantly contemplate how you will help what's to come. You can never have sufficient cash for the future and you will discover that the more that you save, the better you will be ready to live.

Another motivation behind why you must save is for those startling things. Perhaps you will wind up at a crossroads promotion later on. You must decide one way and you really want to realize that you have the cash to conceal the misfortunes that you could come into record of. You will observe that there are parcel of things that will occur, nonetheless, assuming you set aside cash for your future and those lamentable accidents will continuously be covered and you'll have a lot of opportunity to zero in on the things that make the biggest difference, not your cash issues. You will have a lot of opportunity to zero in on the things that you truly care about and not feel sorry for things like cash

Chapter: 8

Instructions to Expand YOUR Inspiration

TO BEING A Group

At the point when you are given a circumstance that develops a gathering you will find that not exclusively will you need to figure out how to function collectively, yet propel each other to fill in collectively. There are such countless things that you must do to get the gathering to meet up, however every one of the group needs some course and initiative. Quite possibly the most effective way that you can spur a group is by coming to the group and being a great audience and communicator. You will likewise need a child to come to the gathering with great administration abilities. Initiatives are difficult to get, nonetheless, you can constantly figure out how to turn into an incredible pioneer by taking a few classes, as well as, courses. At the point when you come to the gathering as a pioneer you will figure out that everybody will see the value toward the path and meet up. The other thing that you should remember is having the option to come to a gathering with initiative, however not tyranny. You would rather not appear to be the supervisor of the gathering, in any case, in the event that you keep the correspondence channel open, there is no great explanation for why you can't recommend your very own thoughts. In the event that you notice that the gathering has gone off course from an undertaking, you can continuously bring the gathering back through different persuasive errands.

A portion of these things could resemble having some time off, investigating the gathering, and in any event, requesting that the others concoct an answer for the gathering. You will likewise need to think of undertaking constantly oriented exercises so that the gathering is persuaded and prepared for the main jobs. You will likewise see that as on the off chance that you look into some errand orientated exercises, you will actually want to control the heading of the gathering and keep the correspondence open. The exercises that you can do will be on the web or from higher positioning col shift and you can track down a lot of thoughts laborers. You will find that you could make up your own exercises since it relies upon the kind of individuals that you are working with and the sort of group that you are separated from. To inspire somebody, you need to track down

it inside yourself to get the group to prevail upon you and to get the inspiration it takes to keep on track. You will see that on the off chance that you are a great pioneer you won't definitely disapprove of group inspiration, however you ought to constantly be pondering the correspondence channels, and how you can impart better inside the group. You will observe that relational abilities are crucial for you to have the option to persuade anybody. You really should figure out how to propel or lead a group, since numerous life illustrations are by and large piece of group. You'll learn many more illustrations in the event that you are in a gathering that can work as one.

You will observe that it is vital as a pioneer for you to have the option to convey clearly and by being in a few groups you'll get the training and preparation of how to be a pioneer. Being a pioneer is a significant privilege and you may very well need to take everything in with an uplifting perspective. Keep in mind, when you are a positive chief then you will be a dad rt of a positive group. What you get from the group is what you need to make due collectively. In the event that you don't give it the significant investment expected to figure out how to propel anyone then the group will come up short

Chapter: 9

Instructions to Expand Inspiration ABOUT BEING Hitched

With regards to inspiration and being hitched, you will observe that there are a few things that will persuade you to wedded and to remain wedded. The primary reasons would be your mate obviously. The second would be your own sentiments. While the third explanation will be those around you that impact your choices. These individuals will be a portion of your dearest companions and relatives. In the first place, you are roused to get hitched and to remain wedded on account of the individual that is with. There are such countless things that this individual will do to propel you to get hitched. The things are basic consistent things, yet it very well may be something like a grin that could persuade one to get hitched. The little things include in a relationship and the little things will seek after you to wed or remain things like the manner in which they take a gander at you, the manner in which they kiss you, the way that they light up a room. These are genuine instances of inspiration that somebody provides for their mate with regards to wedded.

The second explanation that you might become spurred to wed or remain wedded is your sentiments towards your mate and every one of the little things. They will genuinely affect your sentiments and heart. You will feel when all is good and well and when things aren't really correct. You will see that all that will appear to be irritating or exquisite. You will have times when you are dicey, however everybody does. What will spur you the most in your choice to get hitched is assuming you feel like you could cherish the individual for eternity. At the point when you awaken one day stressed that you'll at absolutely no point ever see them in the future, you realize that it is love and that it is perfect. You will observe that affection is extremely odd, yet strong. It is the main explanation you could be propelled to get hitched or stay in a rough marriage. Anyway we will more often than not permit others to inspire your dynamic cycle. With regards to things like loved ones they are quick to either empower or deter the sentiments that you have about things like marriage. We permit ourselves to be roused by others due to our own vulnerability, but you might find that your companions or family will be carrying on with your existence I you permit them to massively affect your choices. you ought to likewise realize that there will be different elements, as well as, a mix of these groups that will urge you to get hitched. The justification for why somebody gets hitched is totally different from another.

The main thing that you can permit yourself to be spurred by is your sentiments, and your mate. The equivalent goes in the event that you are contemplating leaving a marriage. Marriage is no joking matter and you shouldn't permit yourself to trifle with it. You would rather not have your marriage in inconveniences down the line since you were excessively spurred to get hitched. It is feasible to be excessively inspired. That is the point at which you do what you believe and don't permit yourself to completely consider things. Assuming you are truly considering marriage you ought to track down inspiration in yourself and in the relationship. In the event that your mate can't make you genuinely consider an explanation then perhaps they aren't the one. You really want to find the inspiration of marriage from the individual it is that you wish to be pledged to.

Chapter: 10

Instructions to Expand Inspiration ABOUT BEING Perfect

On the off chance that you really want inspiration to be spotless, you are a great deal off than anticipated. You ought to need to be perfect and clean for the way that it reflects upon you. All that you do and all that you don't do thinks about what your identity is. To that end it is vital that you exceed everyone's expectations in trust of getting off the right impression. Impressions are vital, yet somebody just may discount you due to the way that you introduce yourself, your home, your vehicle, and, surprisingly, your work area. When it comes to your work cospace you ought to track down the inspiration In your laborers. Glance around and perceive how your space rates to the others. It may not be that extraordinary of a plan to leave your workspace a wreck by the same token. Remaining clean might be a prerequisite for a task, truth be told. You ought to exhibit clean ways of behaving at work since you would rather not be segregated all things considered. You will find that individuals will get the feeling that you are a good-for-nothing or lay person. You will be telling yourself and the work. W laborers that you simply don't mind an out when it comes to your appearance, you will be passed judgment on considerably harder. Your appearance will say a great deal about what your identity is and the kind of individual you may be.

The people who are unkempt typically get the standing for being filthy and a lazy pig. They would try and think that you are destitute. Do you truly need to have individuals addressing you rather than you being destitute? Undoubtedly not and you ought to involve that for inspiration to tidy yourself up. Likewise, for the people who are single, you will find that the individuals who look unkempt don't get a ton of dates from Saturday night. They as a rule end up alone, truth be told. There will wind up hurt and forlorn from every one of the inconsiderate remarks that individuals could say. You ought to likewise attempt to save your home clean for the purpose that you will have others over to see it. You will see that as a muddled home and being single don't go perfectly if attempting to get a date. You will likewise become discouraged over your place. You will view that as on the off chance that your loft is muddled, you will feel more discouraged and negative. You will find that your self esteem will go into a winding lower turn and in the event that there isn't a justification for you to be perfect, then nothing can propel you. You should track down the inspiration to remain clean and keep your whole world coordinated and together. Those are coordinated and together that land the ideal position and find the individual mate.

 They are ones that turn out to find success. Not neatness brings you all that you need, however the assessment of regard that you get from others when you can get things cleaned. At the point when your office looks great, your manager sees you. At the point when you look great and smell superb you can get the regard from others that you want

To be propelled to be perfect isn't just hard. There are such countless justifications for why you might become spurred, yet it's generally to stay away from difficulties. At the point when you are untidy and unkempt you stand out and that isn't great. Nobody needs nor requires the kind of bad consideration that you will get from being messy. Being spotless has numerous positive effects on life and it assists you with getting further throughout everyday life. Being perfect permits you to find success, personally.

Chapter: 11

Increment Inspiration FOR Good dieting Propensities

For inspiration

for good dieting propensities, you ought to check yourself out. There are countless individuals on the planet who experience the ill effects of heftiness and it can get more enthusiastic in life for the people who are dreary fat. You will that your weight will keep you away from a great deal of encounters, and your dietary patterns will preclude

you from being solid. So many things could rouse an individual to begin eating right, however there are numerous things that keep an individual away from doing things that are solid. The principal reason that individuals view it hard as inspiration to practice good eating habits is the cost of food. Indeed quality food sources really do cost more, yet in the event that you figure out how to remove every one of the desserts and the unhealthy food, then you will truly be setting aside cash. You might feel that you are getting something else for your dollar, yet you truly aren't. To track down the inspiration to spend the cash on quality food is to find self control. In the event that you are nibbler, you clearly will see a distinction in how much food that you have. Be that as it may, on the off chance that you can track down it in you to start a better approach for life then you will unquestionably have the cash for your changing dietary pattern.

The main explanation that you ought to find inspiration for smart dieting is yourself and family. To begin with, you ought to think often about yourself. You ought to think often about the way that you look and feel. At the point when you eat low quality food, despite the fact that it might taste great, you will find that it can push you down. You will likewise see melancholy when you at last set aside some margin to check yourself out. At the point when you could do without how you look you'll become discouraged and start to despise yourself, notwithstanding, assuming that you make the strides now to eat solid you won't ever need to stress over regretting yourself. Concerning the family, you ought to eat well for them. In the first place, you want to set the model and show your family, generally your children, the correct method for attaching to life. Furthermore, you ought to begin to eat good food for the way that food varieties can be dangerous. After long haul eating of undesirable food varieties your heart starts to debilitate. You might be seriously jeopardizing yourself and your family in view of things like strokes, coronary failures, and hypertension. You will observe that your wellbeing isn't simply your very own worry, however your family minds as well. You ought to expand the propensity for eating quality food sources for everything that you could miss due to all the unhealthy food. Once more , it causes wretchedness, yet it likewise holds you back from doing a portion of the things that a typical individual underestimates. There are such countless things that you will miss since you didn't deal with yourself. You will wind up tired constantly and your temperaments will change radically on the grounds that you are not eating right.

There are such countless things that you will miss due to the terrible food sources that you eat and you truly ought to ponder what's to come. Assuming that you really want inspiration for your wellbeing, what's to come is only the spot. Might you at any point envision what could befall you later on in the event that you don't deal with yourself? You might wind up truly harming yourself as well as other people in light of your absence of worry for wellbeing. As a matter of fact, later on, you might wind up kicking the bucket because you didn't eat the right food sources when you had the decision. Keep in mind, practicing good eating habits is a decision that we as a whole ought to make, come what may.

Chapter: 12

Inspiration FOR A Great DAY AT WORK.

It tends to be extremely hard to track down motivation to go to work, let alone to have a great time at work. Nonetheless, you can start your day loaded with inspiration and assurance to have a great time at work. Numerous things bring an individual day over the course of their day, however why let the monotonous routine of things cut you down. You will need to contemplate all the likelihood that the day could bring. The inspiration to have some good times day can start since you have sufficient rest to feel rested. You need to get no less than eight hours of rest so you can awaken feeling revived. For the people who rest pretty much will just observe their day to be a drag. Then, at that point, whenever you have gotten the perfect proportion of rest, you ought to then ponder having something to eat. Consistently begins with a sound and delightful breakfast. This will likewise give you the energy expected to manage the remainder of the day. The key to finding the inspiration for a pleasant day at work isn't permitting anything to cut you down. You not entirely set in stone to have a decent day to have. You need to awaken with the capacity to let things job away from you. You can't be so focused on your day.

You need to track down the inspiration to have some good times inside yourself. You simply need to awaken believing that the world is full of prospects. Truth be told, did you have any idea about that assuming you start your day imagining that today isn't similar to some other day, your day will turn out to be additional common? It is valid! As a result of Karma, you will find that you will return from the world what you give it. The place of Karma is to carry on with a decent existence and consequently, you will have a decent life. Like assuming that you pass a vagrant o n your method for working, in the event that you toss a smidgen of good cause in their direction you'll wind up getting back something from the world that will be positive. Karma propels individuals regularly. For the people who don't have any idea what Karma is; it is the way that the world treats you. Nonetheless, for you to have great Karma you need to carry on with a decent existence. Karma resembles that adage, "What comes around, goes around." In the event that you are not into the entire thing, you might need to ponder giving up for the wellbeing of your own. Certain individuals find it more straightforward to snicker than cry and that goes something similar for work. Individuals find it more straightforward to play out their occupation when they snicker. It is great to surrender to these individuals. Permit somebody to make you a wisecrack or recount to you a story. By associating with others, you'll find the inspiration to look positive over the course of the day. At the point when you find the inspiration disappearing, you might need to contemplate something that has happened to you of late that was charming and afterward utilize that to propel yourself to see the positive qualities in the day. It is difficult to spur yourself, yet assuming you can start the day on the right foot you'll track down that the inspiration to have some good times at work will turn into

more straightforward than ordinary. You'll observe that not exclusively can you rouse yourself to work harder, however to try and carry on with life happily. There are such countless individuals who fear their work, however in the event that you can see the positive qualities in your days then, at that point, you'll have the option to carry on with a much more joyful life and to have some good times at work.

Chapter: 13

The most effective method to Expand Inspiration

AND BE A Mentor

At the point when you are given a circumstance where you are in an influential position, you will need to make the most of it. You will need to attempt to take advantage of the circumstance on the grounds that not exclusively will you gain proficiency with some hard life sores, however you can likewise figure out the manners in which that you can show your administration abilities off. There are so many things that you can do to propel a gathering as the mentor, yet you have to take ownership of certain things first. In the first place, you will need to view the inspiration as a decent mentor in your own abilities. In the event that you can be a decent pioneer and not be a tyrant then you may be prepared for such position, in any case, being a mentor implies more than administration. You need to know how to pay attention to other people and how to speak with others actually. You really want to know how you can enlighten others regarding your thoughts, yet you want to know how to impart your words obviously and successfully with the goal that the message isn't obscured. How you can build your inspiration and be a mentor is extremely basic. You can start to take more positions of authority. At the point when you can, you ought to assume greater liability by requesting to be put in a pioneer job. You will find that you can be a pioneer consistently working.

Assuming that you take the information that you gain from being a functioning chief, you'll view the inspiration as a coach. In any case, not every person has the stuff to be a mentor. You might be anxious to take an instructing position, yet you must know that when you are a mentor you need to provide the group guidance, structure, and a positive emotionally supportive network. You must be everything for a group when you are the mentor. You need to figure out how to persuade your players. With regards to rousing your players, you will see that not every person will become spurred the same way. A few times you should be extreme with your players and different times you should be delicate. It's difficult to advise how to get somebody to learn or become propelled, and for this reason you really want to attempt everything before you surrender. As a matter of fact, you really ought to never abandon a player or you will be abandoning the group. One method for inspiring somebody is to approach that person and have a profound conversation with the person in question. Get some information about the worries that you might have and you then, at that point, need to get some down time to pay attention to them. Everything can be tackled when you set aside some margin to work things out. You'll find that all that will be better when you can give your player one on one time so you can by and by persuade them to arrive at far superior objectives for them and for the group. This is likewise where you'll get the inspiration to improve as a mentor. With every player that you need to converse with aside, you'll figure out how they should be blessed to receive rouse and you'll likewise find ways that you can develop a mentor.

The most effective way for you to track down the inspiration to turn into a group chief or mentor is by rehearsing your relational abilities. Your relational abilities will spur you to take jobs where you are a pioneer since you'll feel great in such a position. You'll rest easier thinking about your identity too. You'll find all the inspiration that you want in yourself to turn into a decent pioneer. You'll gain from your players and they will make you a superior mentor and a superior individual. The main inspiration that you genuinely should be a mentor and pioneer is inspiration inside yourself to turn into a better individual.

Chapter: 14

Inspiration FOR Recuperating Medication Junkies

You might feel that it is not difficult to inspire others, in any case, you will figure out rapidly sufficient that it isn't generally so natural. You will find that you'll experience issues for certain individuals and you also will feel disappointed from not being willing to give them the additional push, nonetheless, you really want to have patients. With regards to spur and empower others you will have rouse and energy yourself first. At the point when you are amped up for things, so will others . You really want to track down it in yourself to persuade yourself to be amped up for something. On the off chance that you can find the fervor, you'll have the option to talk about your thoughts with everyone around you. The primary thing that you will believe should do while attempting to persuade and empower others is to become enthusiastic about something. You will view that as assuming that you come to others with a ton of enthusiasm and fervor they will start to get energized themselves. You may likewise need to contemplate rewards. Despite the fact that it might seem like pay off, you w sick find that numerous administrators will remunerate their laborers and it will in general stimulate and propel them to work harder. Assuming you end up being a mentor of a games group, you will find that these prizes will truly get the group's blood siphoning.

The prizes doesn't have to be a lot, as a matter of fact, the smidgen of an award will in any case get others amped up for the job that needs to be done. Notwithstanding, you additionally should get your players or laborers a lot of help. At the point when you spur you, you want to tell your players or laborers positive remarks. You really want to help them for their endeavors and invigorate them to be better. When they start to see the outcome in their endeavors they will start to spur themselves, however as a pioneer or mentor, you really want to start the cycle with positive knowledge. Assuming you likewise give them something to look at too. forward to, excessive, a prize you will actually want to inspire and stimulate others. Like on the off chance that you let them know how every one of their endeavors will help the organization or for the gathering, individuals are bound to turn out more diligently for the g More often than not, when you start at a major organization they will tell you precisely that you are mean quite a bit to the organization. This is smart since it helps others have a positive outlook on their work and job in the organization.

It propels themselves since t main beneficiary confidence needs are being met. That is something else; you might need to ponder an idea known as Maslow's ordered progression of requirements. You will observe that your laborers or groups are being met. individuals will feel persuaded and invigorated when they have their five essential need In the event that you have your fundamental necessities alongside security needs, social requirements, and confidence needs you'll be set and headed to meet the self completion step of

The hypothesis. In this you'll work for your entire life attempting to be all that you need to be. That's what Maslow shows in the event that you deal with your representative's essential requirements, they will need to improve personally. They will become self persuaded and headed to buckle down for the gathering or organization's objectives. Assuming that you can deal with your workers o r players you will actually want to spur them. You will have a comprehension among you and you'll see that they will turn out more earnestly for the gathering's common objectives. This is the most ideal way you can approach propelling and empowering others to accomplish every one of the objectives of the organization or gathering.

The most effective method to Assemble Inspiration Latently Many individuals will construct inspiration in the work spot or social circumstance latently. This implies that you construct the inspiration almost too easily. There are numerous ways that you can assemble inspiration without knowing it. Some of the time it is only your regular character and once in a while it is simply from all the information that you have about a subject. At the point when you have power you can inspire others late. Authority has a ton of force, nonetheless, you'll observe that there are various kinds of power that you can have over somebody, notwithstanding, ensure that you utilize the ability to emphatically inspire. With regards to your character, you will find that others simply will generally pay attention to you since they like you. As a matter of fact, you will find that they will pay attention to you since they have come to be aware and pay attention to your gut feelings. You have authority over them on account of the way that you can impact others. Others might find that you simply appear to have the right stuff and should have been a pioneer. you will see that assuming you require some investment to effectively know some laborers they will, consequently, regard you and pay attention to you with inspiration.

They will be more disposed to become aroused when you are in light of the fact that you have provided them with a solid premise of a cordial relationship. You character has a great deal to do with inspiration. You can not persuade somebody in the event that you are not the kind of individual that can get others to tune in. You don't necessarily have major areas of strength for a, yet by carving out an opportunity to get to know a portion of individuals who you meet with, you'll have the option to spur them through a bond. Likewise, you will see that you can rouse others through your position. You might have the option to persuade somebody just because you rank higher than them. This is where you have genuine power over them and accordingly reserve the option to let them know how to perform or act at work. When your manager comes around and makes reference for you to follow through with something, do you not necessarily hop right on that? That is the force of power, nonetheless, there are a few distinct sorts of power and you'll find they all can spur others to turn out more enthusiastically for the organization or gathering objectives. On the off chance that you don't have genuine power over somebody, you might have information authority. You have control over others since you know such a great amount about something. For the individuals who can call themselves bosses or scholars of a subject will generally be powerful, a direct result of the way that they know to such an extent. You will view that as in the event that you have unique information over somebody they will check out at you with esteem for inspiration and motivation. You can persuade somebody since they appreciate you.

That is the following way that you can rouse somebody. You can spur somebody since they like you, whether it b e on a well disposed or heartfelt connection, you'll find that they will seek you for guidance and acknowledgment. This authority can spur somebody since they would rather not frustrate you. Sentiments, for example, can be serious areas of strength for extremely the inspiration that you can get somebody can be much more grounded. Not a great explanation, it is that you can spur somebody, you ought to feel blissful realizing that you can persuade somebody. There aren't such a large number of individuals who feel that they matter or mean to anybody. Certain individuals feel that they would never persuade anybody. Inspiration is an extremely useful asset and it ought to be utilized with alertness. You ought to likewise attempt to persuade somebody for their own greatness, and not so much for yours.

Chapter: 15

The most effective method to Fabricate Inspiration

IN OTHERS

Persuading others can be truly challenging and disappointing. You will observe that there are so many individuals who can be inspired effectively and afterward there are certain individuals who need some additional support. You can inspire by having open correspondence and by giving them the help that they need to go after new and better things. With regards to having open correspondence you must have a receptive outlook. You must have the option to pay attention to them. You want to not just pay attention to what others need to say, yet you need to comprehend everything they are saying to you. An incredible relationship, paying little mind to being companions or family, you will find that your bond will get more grounded by having the option to see one another. When you have shared regard and understanding you will actually want to rouse one another. You will also need to ponder the way that you speak with the individual. You should be immediate and strong. You will likewise have to contemplate everything that you might want to share with the individual. You'll likewise see that as assuming that you pick your words before being more clear. e you talk, the message will end

The main thing that you really want to do to persuade somebody is to descend to their level. This implies you need to know what they are accustomed to. Then you need to plunk down and converse with the individual a session how you feel about them. This implies you need to make sense of why you would like them to become propelled. When you can account for yourself then you will actually want to have a shared comprehension. Now that you are talking you might need to lend some support. You should show them and let them know that regardless of what you're there for them. You'll need to show them support in your relationship with them. At the point when they become amped up for something you want to give them the help and support to pursue it. You would rather not impede their inspiration or cut them off. To energize somebody doesn't imply that you advise the person in question what and how to follow through with something. At the point when you energize somebody you provide them some broad guidance and permit them to dominate. With regards to building inspiration in others you will observe that there are a few abilities that you must have to receive your message obviously across. You should turn into a decent communicator. A decent communicator will actually want to tune in and comprehend the words that the individual is saying. They don't rush to make judgment calls, however stand by to talk. Besides the fact that you must be a decent communicator, however you likewise must show restraint.

This implies that you need to allow the individual to say all that they need to and then you need to continue at your own peril and express your real thoughts. This isn't the point at which you blow up or become distraught, in any case, you need to take a gander at things unbiasedly and cautiously so no one's sentiments are harmed. There are many individuals who find it hard to spur others. You might observe that it is disappointing to converse with somebody, yet assuming you find an opportunity to make yourself clear you ought to have the option to spur the person in question and make your relationship more grounded. Inspiration is something that you must be cautious about . You might wind up sounding bossy and obstinate. In the event that you continue at your own risk, you ought to have the option to persuade them effectively. Inspiration can represent the deciding moment of a relationship, however in the event that you go about it in a differential manner you will find that it will help your relationship become more grounded.

Chapter: 16

Inspiration AND Craftsmanship,

HOW TO Make A Good Time For the people who are craftsmen finding motivation can be hard. Individuals lose inventiveness since they don't have something that makes them motivated. Assuming you can find something to cap moves you, the inspiration for your craft will wake up. How might you propel yourself to make tomfoolery, craftsmanship, and works of art? The main thing that you should do is give up. Toss a piece of paper on the floor and leave it. Take a pencil and simply compose, no stressing over what. There are such countless exercises that will get your psyche working and your specialty will simply show up. Everything that you can manage in the event that you have an absence of imagination is to take a piece of paper and a pencil/pen and compose. You can write in sentences, simply words, or meander aimlessly. Assuming you permit yourself to compose automatically, you'll discover a few thoughts. Following a moment or thereabouts, you ought to then peruse what you have composed and you'll doubtlessly discover some sort of motivation to get the inventive energies working. Inspiration is something that you will most likely be unable to create without anyone else. Now and again composing carelessly doesn't necessarily in every case work.

This is the point at which you really want to go out and go for a stroll. Try not to contemplate anything, yet sit in a recreation area or close to a tree and watch life cruise you by. At the point when you notice that you have a lot at the forefront of your thoughts, assuming you can quit everything, you'll have the option to persuade yourself. There is such a lot of motivation in the little things that encompass you. There is a ton of inspiration that you can create from regular day to day existence. Inspiration and craftsmanship is rare. The issue is that you might have an excessive number of thoughts and it doesn't figure out mixing every one of the thoughts together. Assuming it is fun that you are attempting to make, you might need to proceed to have a great time yourself.

You should get out and have a great time. Go out for certain companions to a bar and let go of all the pressure. You can go with your nieces or nephews and have a great time at an event congregation. The basic good times will move you and rouse you to make workmanship loaded up with fun. You find that the great things that you have with others will assist you with giving up the entirety of your pressure and make some superb craftsmanship and have a good time getting it done. For the individuals who are essayists, you'll view that as it's difficult to make fun while attempting to make workmanship.

That's what you'll find assuming you remove a period from your day to zero in on yourself you'll have the option to have some good times making your show-stopper. For the individuals who are painters or drawers, you'll find the inspiration that you really want by investing energy with others and returning to the straightforward life. Life gets confused as we grow up, notwithstanding, on the off chance that we require some investment to have a great time and a crazy time life doesn't appear to be so terrible.

It's great to carry on like a youngster occasionally, in light of the fact that it keeps our brains perpetually turning thoughts out. Good times will rouse you and spur you to assemble something awesome. Likewise, for the people who can involve fun as inspiration or motivation will wind up having a more full life. Assuming you wind up tracking down the things that return you to some piece of your honest adolescence, you will actually want to rouse yourself to make craftsmanship. You'll likewise rest easier thinking about yourself and your capacity to work. Fun immensely affects an individual's soul and the better time that you have the better life gets.

Chapter: 17

HOW Inspiration AND MUSIC Associate

With regards to inspiration, we track down a wide range of things. Your friends, your pet, a film, and even music can spur you. Music has a colossal impact throughout everyday life. Music has animated a large number of individuals to seek after dreams and to track down you. With regards to music, it appears to move those early in life. What music is that it's all over the place and everything. You can hear a tune that has similar verses as another, however sounds totally unique. Music spurs others such that nothing else can analyze. It inspires you to start to feel something from the verses and music of a tune. You'll find that music can modify your temperament. Contingent upon the sort of music you can get siphoned up for a game, you can prepare for bed, you could in fact produce some energy. Music can likewise persuade others what to do. What about music is that it can contact you. You can connect with the music and you can track down solace in the words and notes of a melody. The meager g is that certain individuals permit the music to persuade them in a positive or negative manner.

Contingent upon how you take something, anything can give you a positive or negative thought on life or a piece of your life. You can be roused to be a superior individual from a tune. You can be spurred to let somebody know that you love the person in question. You might try and become inspired to get doing great. How and for what reason does music appear to have such power? Music has power since it tends to be something that we can connect with. It is something that we could possibly comprehend and it gives individuals solace having the option to relate. It causes somebody to feel significant. It causes somebody to feel like there are other people who understand what they are going through and they have chosen to make their life a good one. As we grow up, music turns out to be significantly more essential to us. In the high schooler years, music assists an individual with finding what their identity is. It assists a high schooler with traversing their clumsiness and work towards a positive light. A few times when we go through troublesome things like medication or liquor misuse. The music can contact an individual so profoundly that they have the solidarity to need to change. Music gives an individual mental fortitude. You can not pay attention to the radio each and every day and not wind up roused to follow through with something. You will stand by listening to music and feel something within you change. You'll see that your mind-set will become negative or positive due to a melody.

Music, when completely paid attention to, has more control over are contemplations and sentiments then what your folks or mate could ha ve. Music is a very motivation thing. Have you at any point saw that you work harder and longer when you have the radio on? It has been demonstrated that individuals work harder when music is available than when it isn't. To that end numerous organizations and foundations will give their laborers music. It's not completely specific why individuals are spurred, however it is sure that it makes you arrive at your objectives. It might simply be something to conceal the abnormal quietness, yet it very well may be something in the beat that makes yo u work harder. Music is inspiration regardless of anything. You will find that music makes you start to think and dream. Music likewise jump-starts the system since it empowers others to go about their responsibilities. Assuming music is anything, it is energy. It will get you moving and it can likewise motivate you to improve personally.

Chapter: 18

The most effective method to Involve Inspiration

IN A LETTER

With regards to utilizing inspiration, you can involve it in any type of correspondence. You can involve it in an email, text, verbal correspondence, and furthermore in a letter. In the event that you are contemplating composing a letter to somebody, you ought to ponder utilizing some inspiration. You will view that you are more mindful of the words that you pick in a letter. At the point when we speak with others they utilize the manner of speaking, the words, and non-verbal communication to convey an idea, be that as it may, with a letter you are just utilizing your words. You might have the option to get your sentiments across by making things underwrite, however more often than not you won't have the option to get all that you w subterranean insect across. This is where you really want to express yourself astutely and afterward you'll need to get a few groups to peruse it so the message is clear. The principal things that you will believe should do to compose a letter of inspiration is make an association with the peruser. This is where you keep in touch with some casual chit chat and sort of set out to avoid the real issue. You don't straightforwardly let somebody know that you're stressed or that you're concerned.

You simply need to make an association with the peruser. Whenever you have made the association with the reader you'll need to portray your thought processes in need to motivate them. Make sense of your sentiments and intentions. You might observe that something would better the organization or better the individual's life. Contingent upon the relationship that you have with this person will characterize your rationale. Assuming something would help you, you shouldn't conceal that reality. Assuming this is the sort of thing that would improve your life then you really want to let them know that. You should simply let the individual know that you both have a decent relationship and that you really want some help. Truly what will rouse you to improve personally or follow through with something. Assuming you feel like you are being deceived, you won't be roused to do anything and to that end you should tell the truth. All through the letter you should have the option to remain on point and to steady. You maintain that your words should be immediate and clear. You additionally maintain that your words should seem as though you're tell the truth and worried for their own advantage. You will need to come steady and understanding. Kind words will continuously be a method for inspiring somebody. You can continuously prevail upon somebody with a benevolent word as opposed to a harsh word. You'll likewise view that as assuming that you extend regard, you'll get regard. At the point when you are attempting to rouse somebody through a letter you need to contemplate the regard that is written in the most natural sounding way for you.

Essentially, in the event that you show your anxiety and care for the individual's prosperity you'll have the option to rouse them to improve personally. You can involve inspiration in a letter and for some the letter is the main structure that you can do as such. You will need to ensure that you compose nothing in the letter that you wouldn't believe others should pursue. You ought to likewise contemplate the way that you would have no desire to compose anything that you wouldn't believe somebody should ponder you. This implies that you shouldn't involve profanity or revolting language in a letter. That letter will catch up with you, as well as, composing data that you wouldn't believe others should be aware of. At the point when you express yourself shrewdly, you will actually want to convey the idea and decidedly persuade somebody.

Chapter: 19

WHERE TO FIND Inspiration BOOKS

Is it safe to say that you are searching for inspiration books? Is it safe to say that you are mindful that you can find persuasive books anyplace now? Besides the fact that you can buy a persuasive book at any neighborhood book shop, you can likewise buy them online through different destinations. You can likewise get an inspirational book at the library to buy the book. For those searching for a few inspirational books to buy you w sick need to do it either on the web or disconnected. With regards to finding inspiration books you can go to any of the neighborhood shopping centers or books stores and track down something that you are searching for. Nonetheless, there are such countless inspirational books that you might need to know explicitly the thing you are searching for. You might require an inspirational book to show you how to cook, how to be a superior individual, or how to find another side interest. You'll have the option to track down a book to propel you for anything. At the point when you go to the book shop you wil l need to come by the work area agent and ask where the persuasive or self improvement guides are found. Then, at that point, when you go over and look at the books you might need to see what turns out best for you.

You'll likewise have to ask perhaps for some help or conclusions from the store laborers. You can take as much time as necessary and flick through the book. You will likewise need to ensure that it is precisely the exact thing you are searching for in light of the fact that books truly do will generally be extravagant. For the individuals to have the opportunity to look things up on the net you might need to go to one of the destinations that give you books. Locals like Barnes and Respectable or Amazon.com will assist you with finding the book that you are searching for. The greatest aspect of going on the web to buy a book is that you can pick everything. You can pick your cost (since the two of them will have utilized or new books), and you get to pick the book. A few stores don't offer that numerous choices, however you'll track down a great many inspirational books on these locales. You will need to ensure that you read a couple of pages of the digital book, as well as, check the survey out. You'll have the option to track down the right book for yourself despite everything in the delight of your own time. You can travel every which way to find the right book and you don't need to feel like you're being raced to make a buy.

You might all at any point so have the book sent straightforwardly to your home or you can get the book at a nearby Horse shelters and Respectable, nonetheless, you will find that getting the book is more helpful for yourself. Presently persuasive books can be exorbitant. You will observe that there are a great deal of books that you will have added to your assortment and you could reach the place where you simply don't need another book laying around.

For that reason individuals utilize the library. You can utilize the library regardless of how old you are. There are a lot of libraries that will send books in from different libraries, on the off chance that they don't have what you are searching for. It's good to utilize the library since you're not paying the cash for the book. You are additionally rewarding the local area on the grounds that each time that you utilize the library administrations you will wind up making the library and the local area cash through reserves. Up to a library being utilized the public authority (nearby and state) will reward the offices.

Chapter: 20

WHAT IS Inspiration

What's really going on with It? How could it at any point help you and where does it come from? These are only a portion of the inquiries that will be responded to. Inspiration is something that drives you from within. A sensation of feeling will drive you to take a stab at objectives and accomplish all of the slight that you might want to do. It comes from inside your heart. It comes from the spot of your heart that makes you need to be a superior individual. Keeps mankind pushing ahead with inspiration. Inspiration can do a great deal for an individual. It can assist an individual with accomplishing an objective short term or long haul. It can assist an individual with tracking down themselves. It can likewise assist an individual with improving personally. With regards to inspiration you can do anything that you like to do. It drives you to be a superior individual since it allows you to develop and to learn. Inspiration permits you to dare to characterize yourself and to connect and search out new encounters. You will wind up growing a great deal as an individual since you permit yourself to encounter new things beyond your solace zone. At the point when you remove yourself from your usual range of familiarity you will find that you can have love, tomfoolery, achievement, and all that you can at any point ponder.

Self inspiration is the best inspiration that you can have, in any case, you can become roused by different things. You can be roused by your friends, your friends and family, and your religion. With regards to self inspiration you will find it inside yourself a strong energy gloat to go for what you need. This energy brag won't permit you to stop until you have had your objective. Self inspiration is the best only for the way that you are doing it for yourself. You're not changing or going after better standards as a result of another person, however you are basically doing it for your better great. Self inspiration can likewise b e the most remarkable type of inspiration. Many decided individuals will be engaged to such an extent that they will simply not surrender or quit. Once in a while it can seem like you're marginal over the top, nonetheless, you will feel so effective when you arrive at an objective in light of self inspiration. Individuals are additionally known to be roused by different things. You can be inspired by another person or cash. At the point when another person rouses you it is for the most part since you are being compelled to. You are generally propelled in light of the fact that they give you a final proposal. They give you a decision and you feel compelled to change or you will wind up rebuffed. This isn't generally the most ideal way to get yourself moving. Notwithstanding, in the event that somebody is attempting to rouse you, you ought to figure the reason why and attempt to track down a method for spurring yourself.

Presently individuals say that they are spurred to work due to the cash. In any case, cash isn't the main justification for why you are persuaded to work. Regardless of whether you assume you are roused to work due to the cash, it is additionally so you can feel total. Individuals are propelled for the most part so they can feel good. Certain individuals consume their whole time on earth attempting to find something that will inspire them, however the whole response exists in. Individuals are inspired in view of so many reasons and inspiration can do so many for an individual's inner self, confidence, and profession due to all the achievement that you will find. Achievement is a major brag to the self image and with a smidgen of self inspiration objectives can be reached thus will such countless more future objectives.

Chapter: 21

Inspiration FOR Representatives HOW TO Kick IT Off

There are so many ways that you can spur an individual, notwithstanding, you need to ponder the individual and their character before you attempt to propel representatives. It's great that you need to spur your laborers since you will ultimately work on your creation and afterward benefit. There is a ton to acquire with roused workers, in any case, you really want to know how to get them persuaded. With regards to inspiration you should be sure about your remarks towards the representatives. Each one is unique and should be dealt with in an unexpected way. There are a couple of ways that you can propel your workers. The primary way is their commendations and ideas. This is where you give them consolation by praising their efficiency and afterward you recommend for them to define another objective or backing them to keep on arriving at their objectives. This is the way that you really want to treat delicate laborers. You can inspire them since they need a tiny bit of gloat to their confidence to be somewhat wagered ter. The subsequent way is to give strong analysis. There are certain individuals who are sticklers and when you give them helpful analysis, you can rouse them to perform better

What you are doing is provoking them to go after a more significant level execution or objective setting. The third method for spurring a laborer is forcibly or power. This isn't recommended, yet in the event that nothing else occurs, they will begin to work harder assuming they realize that they are being checked. Assuming they realize that they are in the rundown of individuals who might actually be terminated, they will work harder than any time in recent memory. Quite possibly the main instrument that you should spur your laborers is empowering words. You should show your laborers that you care about their own objectives as well as the organization's objectives. You should have the option to show your laborers that you really care about their advancement. Then you ought to ponder the power. Try not to permit yourself to be a harasser. If you truly have any desire to get your laborers to turn out to be better, you will need support and understanding. ve In the event that you observe that you are losing your patients with a laborer, you might need to put down and converse with that specialist. Through the talking, you will track down inspiration for the both of you. You will actually want to find something that will push the laborer to their true capacity and you will likewise get a superior comprehension of how to move toward the specialist later on. Inspiration is something that comes from all over the place. It comes from the board, it comes from companions, and it comes from inside. Numerous businesses settle on some unacceptable choice to give things to them

 Giving gifts as rewards to the employees is just nice every now and then. It is appreciated by employees if you give them a gift every now and then.

In the event that you notice that your laborers aren't giving you what you really want, then, at that point, you might need to challenge them by offering a prize. You will likewise need to utilize this strategy when you arrive at an impasse. At the point when you have had a go at all the other things, prizes will work out. This can be a little raise, a three day weekend paid, an additional excursion day, etc. Simply give them something little that will flaunt their morals so they can do their absolute best with it. This is a method for kicking the inspiration off in your working environment, nonetheless, with a couple of kind words, and some support and understanding, you can have extraordinary representatives.

Chapter: 22

Inspiration FOR Kids, HOW TO Show THEM critical

it is that inspiration is introduced in your youngster since it is the premise of their confidence. Youngsters should be persuaded and upheld by their folks so that when they grow up, they can pursue the ideal choices. It's difficult to show your kids things like inspiration, nonetheless, you can show your kid how to be self propelled. Self spurred kids grow up to be self propelled grown-ups. The main thing that you can accomplish for your kids is let them know that you love them. Let them know exactly the amount you give it a second thought and back their objectives. Let them know that they will continuously be your youngsters regardless. In any case, with this showcase of affection you want to tell them that it's perfect to have objectives, yet urge them to permit themselves to return to others as needs be. The most awesome aspect of showing your kids how to rouse themselves is showing your youngsters exactly the amount you give it a second thought. Tell them that for some time they have a wellbeing net with regards to the world. Urge them to characterize what their identity is and what they need. They support them at whatever point they need you. You really want to help your kids regardless of your thought process.

There will be a few mix-ups that they make en route, yet for however long they aren't significant then you don't have to meddle. In the event that it doesn't end up working, the kids will learn. With regards to growing up our mix-ups have the greatest effect on our lives. The most horrendously awful thing that you can do is choke out your kid. You can't spur your kid on by providing them guidance. You really want to give them a little help and through the nurturing that you have done, you ought to find that they would go with the ideal choice. At the point when you settle on the decisions for them you are not rousing them. You are pulverizing their confidence and capacity to be independent. There are a ton of guardians that commit that error, notwithstanding, on the off chance that you require some investment to converse with your kid about their decisions in their day to day existence, you are giving them ethics to live by and that will spur them to improve personally. Something else that you would rather not do is judge your kids due to their choices. At the point when you start, passing judgment on them due to a choice that they made will deter them from standing freely and it will hurt their confidence. Inspiration needs self esteem in light of the fact that they need to dare to go for something that they love or appreciate. With regards to nurturing, you want to support them. At the point when you support them they will track down it inside to spur themselves with the goal that they can grow up to freely turn into.

It's difficult to show your kids and it tends to be truly challenging, in any case, assuming you let them know that you love them and assuming you let them know that they will constantly be your youngsters. Work things out with your kid so they can track down solace and backing in your inspiration. At the point when you are spurring your kid, ensure that you give them a lot of choices so they can feel free and you can persuade the kid to go after far superior objectives. At the point when you are rousing your kid you want to recollect that you mean a lot to their life. You are the focal point of the universe and you need to start a trend by being a decent good example. By being a decent good example and strong of your kids, you will track down that your kids will become self propelled and free.

Chapter: 23

Inspiration FOR YOUR Mate, HOW TO Persuade YOUR Life partner

For the inspiration of one self is hard, it tends to be significantly more diligently on the off chance that you are attempting to spur your companion. You not just need to show them that you give it a second thought and back them, yet you likewise need to contemplate their sentiments. Could you at any point inspire your life partner without hurting your relationship? There are a ton of ladies and men who attempt to persuade their mates and end up single. Why would that be? More often than not they turn out to be single since they push too hard. You need to give a push and you maintain that your life partner should become persuaded, yet there is where your inspiration strategy can turn out to be irritating. At the point when you start to pester your mate that is the point at which you start to lose their regard and love. With regards to empowering your mate you need to ensure that you have a common regard for one another. Once you have that regard you can inspire your mate without making it a threatening circumstance. The initial step to empowering or inspiring is supporting. You need to let the individual know that you will assist them with arriving at their objectives by supporting them and empowering them to be a superior individual. You won't just need to discuss their sentiments, yet your sentiments also.

At the point when you discuss your sentiments and the manner in which you see the relationship or circumstance. Then you want to discuss what it is that they should be urged to do. At the point when you discuss inspiration, you really want to know how they feel about the circumstance. At the point when you open the correspondence channels you will find what is happening will be more straightforward to deal with and they won't feel like you are being pushy . You must be cautious with regards to empowering your mate. You don't need a tad of empowerment to turn out to be some large colossal battle. At the point when you energize your mate you maintain that it should appear to be not so much controlling but rather more concerning. You will need to ensure that you talk over things. Additionally, you want to contemplate the way that you talk. The status quo is vital. You can take something that is to seem like a commendation, yet it tends to be taken like an affront. The way that you make statements incorporate your manner of speaking and the words that you pick, so express yourself carefully so you don't wind up lamenting whatever that you say. Likewise, set aside some margin to make a comprehension and talk about your requirements. Empowering a mate is extremely hard. It is hard in light of the fact that you are so near this individual and you would rather not put them in a horrible mood or cause them to feel terrible. When you have the premise of the comprehension since both of you have talked, you will need to ensure that you utilize your words and activities to show them that you have all aims of supporting and cherishing them regardless.

You will find that you can propel or empower your mate by letting them know that you love them and need them. Convince them to go after far superior thoughts . You will actually want to construct areas of strength for a solid relationship and you can likewise have a confident and free accomplice too. Inspiration means quite a bit to your organization and relationship. Your relationship will actually want to push ahead and keep on pushing ahead flawlessly on the grounds that both of you have tracked down ways of persuading yourself and make the relationship more grounded.

The most effective method to Build YOUR Inspiration TOWARDS YOUR FAMILY Having great inspiration towards your family is significant. You want to pursue the choice to build your inspiration with the goal that you can have a more joyful and better everyday life. This is the kind of thing that will lead you to a superior coexistence. This is the kind of thing that most everybody needs to have in their life. A blissful family that connects together and has a great deal of adoration to spread around will be more grounded than one that doesn't. You want to contemplate how you might build your inspiration towards your loved ones. Ponder that they are so vital to you and how you would feel if at any time you didn't have them. You would feel horrible and it is something that you would have zero desire to have occur. You want to see the value in what you have with the goal that you can exploit it. You really want to begin to talk more to your family as well. This will assist you with remaining engaged with the things that happen in their lives. You will actually want to catch wind of one another's day and all the significant and non happened to them. significant things that have

You will feel nearer to your family since you are discussing things that you have never discussed. This is an extraordinary move toward getting spurred towards your family somewhat more. Hanging out is just about the most ideal way to get more inspiration towards your loved ones. You want to simply invest some quality energy following through with something or doing nothing by any stretch of the imagination. You don't have to have a timetable arranged to invest some energy with your loved ones. You should simply be in a similar room together. Nowadays it is difficult to get everybody all together simultaneously. You need to take what you can and afterward develop it into arranging occasions that all of you can do together. Do things that all of you can like together. You shouldn't reject one individual out of the good times. You want to all pick something that will unite you and permit you all to have a great time simultaneously. You can likewise design an extraordinary family excursion with one another. This is the sort of thing that all of you can do together and have an awesome time making it happen. The primary thing that you ought to do is ensure that everyone can go simultaneously and afterward pick a spot that everybody will like. It doesn't need to be costly to do this by any stretch of the imagination. Truth be told you can go anyplace for however long you are together and this will expand your family inspiration. Try not to fear your loved ones. They are the main things in your day to day existence and when they are gone, you will be heartbroken. You need to design now for time together so you are getting every one of the advantages that you can from a family. There isn't anything better than having

somebody to share the great and the terrible times with and family is disobediently going to show up for you when you are out of luck. Expanding your inspiration towards your family ought to be something that you maintain that you should do and lighthearted about doing. You will see that you can have an incredible day to day life and not need to stress over passing up a major opportunity any longer. You will feel better realizing that you have done all that you can with regards to being roused with your family and in the end they will see the value in it as well.

Chapter: 24

The most effective method to Build Inspiration YOUR Inspiration

is something that we as a whole must have. We as a whole need to find the right degrees of inspiration in our life so we can do our desired things and have a great time doing them. Nothing bad can really be said about needing to have more inspiration in your life. You can expand your inspiration and carry on with a more joyful and better way of life. You won't need to stress over how hard this will be on the grounds that there are a couple of things that you can do to make it go significantly quicker for you. You want to ask you for yourself a few significant inquiries when you are looking inspiration.

You want to ponder what you ought to do and what you are doing. How can you go to feel on the off chance that you don't get something achieved throughout everyday life? Furthermore, what you need to keep on doing in your life to remain cheerful? These are everything that you ought to ask yourself first and afterward this will decide whether you really want to build your inspiration about something specific or not. You need to begin pursuing dynamic decisions in your day to day existence. You want t o have a force of psyche that will permit you to do the things that you like to and not let anything hold you up.

Assuming you say that you will follow through with something, you want to ensure that you see everything through to completion. This is the main way that you can finish things in your day to day existence that will fulfill you eventually. At the point when you feel as though you have achieved something, you will feel significantly improved on the grounds that you did what you needed to. Put forth objectives for yourself to expand your inspiration. You will need to contemplate your desired activities and afterward the way that you can finish them. Ensure that you are laying out reasonable objectives for yourself. Try not to make them something difficult to do. You need to set long haul and momentary objectives so you can have at some point to achieve as you go. These objectives can assist you with getting in good shape so you stay there with your inspiration. Get great good examples to trail not too far behind. You will find that when you admire somebody that is doing great in their self motivation, this will assist you with accomplishing yours. You will find it more straightforward to do your desired things since you will get them going. You will have a lot to gain by going for it and you will have the motivation of the good examples to follow you. You will feel better and realize that you can do it since you have the strength and the power behind you to make it happen. Understand what you need and don't need throughout everyday life. There are things that will change as you fill throughout everyday life. You won't have similar objectives and you will need to meaningfully alter the way that you check specific things out.

This checks out. Everything that you can manage is remaining positive and understands what you need and how to get it. Center around each thing in turn and afterward happen from that point. At the point when you get one dainty g cultivated, this will assist you with keeping your inspiration and continue to continue on down the line. Be grateful for the things that you have throughout everyday life. You need to ensure that you don't underestimate things and value the things that you have around you. You need to ensure that you are keeping an uplifting perspective on things that you as of now have and the objectives that spur you to continue to go throughout everyday life. You have such a huge amount to be thankful until further notice and consider what you can do on the off chance that you continue to go with your inspiration. You can have an extraordinary life loaded up with limitless open doors on the off chance that you keep your inspiration the correct way.

Chapter: 25

Inspiration Strategies FOR Little kids, Techniques THAT Rouse

You really want to attempt to propel your kids however much you can. This Is the equivalent for little kids. They all should be shown the right strategies for inspiration and how to continue to go through anything. Such countless little kids lose interest in things since they don't have the right inspiration driving them. There are a few things that we can do as guardians and coaches to assist them with remaining in good shape and finish things that they start. Keeping little kids on the right inspiration strategies is vital to do. Try not to annoy your youngster. You ought to attempt to stop the irritating that daily to you do on day premise with your little kid. You ought to rather attempt to get them persuaded with your words. Pestering can cause them to feel awful like they misunderstand entirely followed through with something. You need to get them roused to do what you maintain that they should do or w cap they have laid out as objectives for themselves. You will see that you will get to a greater extent a decent response from them when you are inspiring them and not continually pestering and coming down on them.

Offer them a chance to commit their own errors. You need to proceed to allow them to do what they believe they need to. Some will succeed and others will fall flat. Everything revolves around doing what is significant and realizing the message that you won't ever be aware until you attempt. Attempting is the most ideal sort of inspiration. At the point when they really do commit an error, let the little kid in on what she attempted and that is overwhelmingly significant. Tell her that she should keep roused and attempt once more for the things that she truly needs to have throughout everyday life. Give them instances of others that are roused and everything that they have achieved. This is the sort of thing that ought to assist them with accomplishing their objectives and getting done great. At the point when you have the motivation around you to do beneficial things, you will have a superior shot at them since you have the power and the strength surrounding you. Getting persuaded is something that you can do whenever you feel that you want a tad of help finishing something. You will just advance beneficial things from the models that are tossed your direction. Instruct young young ladies self-esteem. This is the kind of thing that we should do to get them aroused throughout everyday life. We need to tell them that they are esteemed and they have significant activities. Inspiring them to comprehend that they have a great deal of self-esteem will make it simpler for them to accomplish objectives that are vital to them and permit them the opportunity to win or lose. They must have the inspiration to need to attempt and by instructing them that they are worth so much, they won't be hesitant about attempting.

Showing little kids to b e roused now will help them as they become and progress in years. They will have the right self-assurance that they need to do and attempt what they need. They will have the solidarity to trust in their desired things and to feel better about any choice that they might have later on from now on. Preparing them very early on for autonomy is significant and inspiration goes right alongside that. You need to settle on them mindful of the decisions that they will have and that each young lady and ladies has the option to make her own brain up. This is a power that they will take with them for a lifetime.

Chapter: 26

Inspiration Techniques FOR Little fellows,

Strategies THAT Rouse

Your youngsters are your most noteworthy objective throughout everyday life. You need to ensure that you are taking care of your business as a parent with regards to propelling them into individuals that they are and doing what they believe they should do throughout everyday life. You need to attempt to show them inspiration abilities when they are young men with the goal that they can keep doing great throughout everyday life. You really want to show them that they can be propelled throughout everyday life and that there are things to be amped up for. You need to show little fellows that they are significant throughout everyday life. You can give them the devices that they should do the things that they like to. You can show them that they don't need to be reluctant to attempt new and fascinating things. Give them the assets that they need to explore the objectives in life that they need to have. At the point when they find out about things they will be expanding their inspiration towards them. Permit them the change to develop and get these valuable open doors. Show restraint toward your little fellow. You must have the option to give them an opportunity to deal with their inspiration. This isn't something going to come to them overnight. You might need to convince them to refocus.

This is the same old thing. You must have the persistence to permit them the opportunity to succeed and to come up short. You don't need to push them at the same time to be persuaded. It will come in time and you will see it when all is good and well. Showing young men that it is vital to have objectives very early in life will allow them the opportunity to need to prevail at them. This consequently will permit them to need to have more objectives as they go. Reaching the place where they will get the opportunity to go out and do the things that are critical to them is what you need. You need them to not be reluctant to have dreams and to pursue them. Give them the push that they need to spur them. Allow them to play part models. Allow them the opportunity to admire somebody that is positive. Permit them to have the opportunity to have somebody that they need to be like. This will give them a few inspiration towards life and every one of the potential outcomes that are out there. They can persuade eager to resemble somebody that they gaze upward at.

This will show them that when you have dreams they can materialize when you buckle sufficiently down. Allow them to have exercises that they need to do. This will keep them keen on something that can help them over the long haul. You believe they should attempt new things and find the ones that they are great at. At the point when a little fellow is great at something they will feel significantly better about what their identity is and what they have accomplished through it.

Be positive with the little fellows in your day to day existence and show them that the sky's the limit. Having the right perspective is significant. Additionally train them to avoid the negative things in life that can bring them down some unacceptable street. You believe that they should be aware of the terrible things so they are not convinced by others to attempt them. This will be something that will assist them with accomplishing just beneficial things and it will keep them inspired to continue to examine their own objectives.

Chapter: 27

Inspiration Techniques FOR Unseasoned parents,

Strategies TO Propel

Being another parent is something that can be scary from the outset. You may not understand what you ought to do and how you can be the most ideal parent. The main way that you can learn is by doing your thought process correctly and afterward gaining from your errors. You must be spurred to continue to attempt and t o do all that can be expected. Viewing better approaches to propel you as a superior parent isn't simple all the time. You need to remain with it and you will see that the prizes will come. . We as a whole need to be a decent parent. The best way to do this is to learn on our own. We will pursue great and terrible decisions anyway; being a parent is something that doesn't accompany a guidance manual and thus we need to make it up as we go. Being roused to be the best is one method for being a decent parent and to show our youngsters that they are the main inspiration in our life. You are responsible for another life when you are another parent. You are the one that will be answerable for this individual. You really want to give your very best to cause them to turn into all that You need to buckle down regularly when you are a parent. You should be prepared for this new test in your life. Getting spurred is the most effective way to do this. You need to be geared up for any eventuality and you will be the point at which you are ready. Getting prepared is something that you ought to contemplate. How might you be ready to be another parent? Once in a while there are no responses, you will simply need to follow what is in your heart, and your thought process is the most effective way. Consider this new kid that has entered your life. You believe you should do all that can be expected for themselves and this will incorporate your very own objectives. You need to rouse yourself to improve in the vocation that you have and every one of the objectives that you have set for yourself along these lines. You need to make the best life for your kid and this will incorporate genuinely as well as truly as well. Take counsel from others that are around you. You can gain some useful knowledge from your companions that are now guardians. You can get inspired from their energy and take various examples from them. You don't need to essentially follow their nurturing abilities, however you can take each growth opportunity and utilize that in your own nurturing technique. There is no set in stone when you are a parent. You should simply follow your inspiration and see where it leads you. Become amped up for being a parent and utilize your sentiments to make this work for you.

Ponder what you wanted as you were growing up. Did you have the ideal adolescence or were there things that you could change? You can gain from quite a while ago and utilize these things to assist you with being more inspired to be your desired parent to be. Get some margin to contemplate what might have helped you more when you were a kid and utilize these models when you become a parent. Recall that you don't need to be great and as a matter of fact you will commit errors. Anyway all great guardians gain from their slip-ups and continue on toward the following experience in nurturing that is hanging tight for them.

Chapter: 28

Inspiration Techniques FOR NEW Mothers, TO GET YOU Rolling

Being another mother is an extremely interesting and startling experience for some. It is something that you need to find out about as you go. There is absolutely not a chance of realizing what will occur from now on and you must be ready for anything that comes your direction. Being a decent mother implies that you must have the right inspiration to learn and attempt new things. You can do this with the right strategies and eventually; you will be a propelled mother that will do anything for the new minimal one in her life. New mothers can find extraordinary strength in the way that they are currently in control of human existence. Getting enlivened from this is the best objective that a mother can have. It means a lot to need to be all that you can be and with this will come numerous things. You should succeed and flop simultaneously. Committing errors when you are another mother checks out. Anyway you need to gain from them and afterward continue on. Gain from others. You can glean tons of useful knowledge from other mothers that have experienced all that you have. Taking guidance from these mothers checks out.

You can decide to do everything they say to you or you can make it up as you go. You don't need to follow their methods to the T. You can think twice about close to nothing and add your own exceptional inventiveness to your nurturing abilities. You can get spurred through this technique and use it as an opportunity for growth to be an extraordinary mother. Having objectives for what's in store is critical to. You might have things that you need to achieve with your kid as you go. Make both present moment and long haul objectives. Anyway you would rather not blow up in the event that these objectives don't work out as you plan .You need to permit yourself space to commit errors and for things to be slowed down in time a bit. A few circumstances don't pan out as we plan constantly. The equivalent goes for being another mother. Things will come up constantly and these will be essential for life. Nothing remains at this point but to remain roused to be doing great and you will see that things will turn out for you eventually. Try not to become too stirred up over things when you are another mother. You need to understand that things will occur and you don't necessarily in every case have the responses. At the point when this occurs, you can figure out how to improve things. You should simply put stock in your power as a mother and you will find the solidarity to make all that work out. You might not have the right response constantly, however you want to permit yourself the chance to be off-base and to gain from it.

Having a good time is something significant when you are another mother. Having some good times will persuade the giggling in your life. You need to keep on the good track so you are not permitting yourself to feel awful. You need to play around with your family and value the great times that you can have with them. Not all things will be fun constantly, however you want to realize that you can have a great time and give up as needs be. This will assist with saving you persuaded in the correct bearing for being a mother and seeing what the future may bring to you.

Chapter: 29

USE Inspiration TO BECOME Dynamic AND EXERCISE,
HOW TO Get more fit

Shedding pounds is something that you need to work at. You really want to ensure that you are giving your best to make this objective work out as expected for yourself.

You must be spurred to get thinner. At the point when not entirely settled to impact the manner in which you look, you will feel improved in light of the fact that you are accomplishing something great for your wellbeing and for the way that you feel about yourself. Getting persuaded to shed pounds is something that you can do with a couple of basic hints. You need to prepare to assume responsibility for your life and do what you need to lose a specific measure of weight. You want to contemplate how you need to make this objective materialize. You might need to sort out a method for scaling back specific food sources or to sort out a successful activity plan. These are only a couple of things that can assist you with getting in shape and feel perfect. Inspiration can be an extraordinary power in your fight to get thinner. You want to become amped up for shedding pounds and getting your body in shape. There are many individuals that don't know how to set propelled up to do this.

You want to ponder the sort of life that you need to have. Does this life incorporate getting more fit and feeling great about how you search in your garments? Provided that this is true, you ought to contemplate how you really want to shed pounds and get your life on the correct path. Becoming roused about something is an incredible method for getting that objective going for you. Doing exercise isn't always something that we need to do. As a matter of fact, many individuals put off doing exercise since they imagine that it is excessively hard. Be that as it may, practice is an extraordinary method for making your objective of getting in shape happens much quicker. You can take care of business since you can practice as indicated by your arrangement and get in shape that is overloading you. Consider the delayed consequences of what you will have when you are propelling your body to get going and get in shape. You will be taking on a test that you have for practically forever needed t o. This is a test that you can have the triumph of winning the skirmish of getting more fit whether it is a couple of pounds or a ton of weight. Find a normal that will turn out better for yourself and stick to it. You want to contemplate the best time you can exercise and what you need to do. You really want to contemplate the regions that you want to work on and afterward utilize that to make up your activity plan. Getting persuaded to shed pounds is something that you can do with a tiny bit of desire. You don't have to invest a great deal of energy into this since all you truly need is the mentality to get you where you need to be with your weight and with your wellbeing.

You don't need to stress over shedding pounds when you have the necessary inspiration to arrive. You can have an effect in the manner that your body looks and the way that you feel when you choose to lay out an objective for yourself. You will be a more joyful individual and you will see the way that a tad of inspiration can completely change yourself to improve things. It will require a smidgen of investment, yet getting spurred for one thing can lead into numerous other incredible objectives that you set for yourself. Gradually you will see that having objectives and inspiration is smart for progress of any sort.

Chapter: 30

Step by step instructions to Utilize Inspiration TAPES

There are numerous things out there to assist you with tracking down your way to inspiration. You can utilize inspiration tapes to get you in good shape. Utilizing these tapes is an extraordinary method for assisting you with making the progress in life that you are searching for. The primary thing that you need to do is sort out the thing you are searching for and afterward get the right kind of tapes to assist you with your objective. Utilizing the inspiration tapes is something that you will just profit from. You will actually want to find inspiration tapes for pretty much any idea that you can imagine. Regardless of what you are hoping to work on in your life, you can track down the ideal tapes to help you. There are audiotapes and there are tapes to get you in good shape for progress in your desired objectives. Investigate what there is out there for you to look over and afterward settle on your choice in view of the determination. You really want to involve the tapes as they are coordinated. You might have to tune in or watch the tapes a couple of times each week to get the full impact of what their motivation is. You need to follow the bearings with the goal that you can advance however much you can to kick your inspiration off.

With the right use, you will see that these inspiration tapes can assist you with getting to where you should be throughout everyday life and with every one of the objectives that you need to accomplish. Numerous inspiration tapes are there to assist you with overseeing your life. You can utilize these as a manual for get you in good shape. You really want to ensure that you can make these tapes work for you so you can transform your life into what you believe it should be. Getting persuaded can assist you with numerous things that you might go through. You can utilize these tapes to assist you with accomplishing specific objectives and to likewise assemble your life back after you have had a terrible encounter.

You can profit from these tapes to assist you through issues that you might have had with pretty much anything that you can imagine. There are inspiration tapes that will assist you with your weight or assist you with making progress throughout everyday life. A portion of the inspiration tapes are also there to assist you with getting more cash and to get your life back to where you maintain that it should be.

You can glean some significant knowledge from the different material that is found on the inspiration tapes. You can pay attention to them in your extra time or make this an everyday daily practice to assist you with traversing terrible times. You don't need to approach something all alone. You can roll out an improvement in your existence with a little assistance from some inspiration tapes that are available. You really want to exploit the ones that will influence your life and the circumstances that you are in.

There are many individuals that don't know whether these inspiration tapes work or not. The best way to truly know is assuming that you attempt them for yourself. You might wind up one of the numerous that have a decent involvement in these tapes and change their life perpetually for a long term benefit. The best way to tell is to attempt it. When you see how you can manage the inspiration that you learn you will have an extraordinary outlook on what your identity is and what you prevail in forever.

Chapter: 31

About Inspiration IN THE HOME Keeping

your home chugging along as expected is really smart. You need to make things fill in however much you can with everybody in the home. You want to consider ways that you can get everything in the functioning request that you want it to be. You might need to work somewhat more diligently at it; however , with the right inspiration abilities, you can keep your home running perfectly and keep everybody persuaded to keep it that way. Inspiration in the house is something that can keep everybody on a timetable. You can ensure that everything gets worn out when it should and that everybody is doing their part to make it work. You want to do things that will permit everybody in the family to keep in good shape and to finish things the way that they should be so all the housework and needs are finished when they should. You don't need to be somebody that is amped up for keeping the family running great. You should simply have a smidgen of the right inspiration to make all the difference for it. You can figure out how to do this from things like inspiration tapes or from somebody who has been there and understands how necessities to got this going for you.

Keeping everybody feeling great in the house is a major assistance. You want to figure out what compels everybody to stay blissful and attempt to keep them in this mind-set. You will see when they are cheerful; they will help out around the house and keep things in the right working order. Get your kids roused to help you around the house. You can likewise utilize a similar kind of inspiration to hold you closer together too. This is the best thing about inspiration. You can involve it for anything that you need to and you will generally witness a constructive outcome. There isn't anything better than seeing something work for the better around you. You ought to show your kids that they don't need to really regret what they do throughout everyday life. Get them persuaded to do so effectively and utilize these sentiments to get a greater amount of what they need throughout everyday life. Utilizing your inspiration abilities is something that you can do to make your home a blissful spot. Use what you know to make your home a welcome spot for other people. You will see that when individuals feel appreciated in your home, they will be more joyful and need to come see you more. You can likewise utilize these abilities to get your family to assist you with things that you will be unable to do all alone. You can utilize your inspiration around the house to get others to assist you with the things that you want them to. You will see that when everybody cooperates, things will finish quicker and simpler with less work.

You don't need to continuously satisfy individuals in your home. You truly do anyway need to keep objectives on target and to utilize what you have realized with inspiration to finish what you really want. You will have a more joyful and more coordinated home when you are taking inspiration and involving it for positive things to occur in your home and around you. This is an objective that you can put out there for your entire family to partake in and you will be resistant to partake in the final products that you have.

Chapter: 32

Inspiration AND YOUR Profession Vocation

inspiration is something incredible to have and on the off chance that you don't have it, you ought to deal with getting it. You really want inspiration to get what you need throughout everyday life and to have the best vocation that you can have. Assuming you believe that you are deficient in inspiration, you want to chip away at it. There are a couple of tips that will assist you with getting to where you should be in your vocation inspiration abilities. There are a couple of basic things that you can do to make it somewhat simpler to get where you need to be throughout everyday life. Contemplate a couple things. Are you content with yours

HOW TO Get more fit

Ponder the drawn out things that you believe you should do and pursue your fantasies. Assuming you have objectives set for yourself later on in the distance, you will see that you can make a solid effort to take care of business. You can utilize your professional inspiration for getting to where you need to be throughout everyday life and in your desired vocation to accomplish. You can have the vocation that you have for a long time truly needed regardless of whether you believe that you it is unimaginable at this moment. There is generally time to get it going and you should simply have vocation inspiration and assurance.

Chapter: 33

Inspiration AND Achievement Techniques

Having inspiration and achievement are two things that go together. You must have one to have the other. The way to having great achievement is how much inspiration you put behind it. You want to have your own thoughts and objectives and afterward figure out how to completely finish them. You want to get an arrangement and afterward set it in motion to make it work. There are various variables in deciding the amount of progress you possess throughout everyday life and how you get spurred. Getting motivation to finish your inspiration and your objectives is significant.

You really want to contemplate what you need and need throughout everyday life. Having an inside objective is something that you can have for your very own prosperity. Contemplate your desired things throughout everyday life and how you mean to inspire them to occur for you. You really want to have personal development and objectives for yourself to make your life mean something. Giving your inspiration abilities something to do in this space will be a colossal advantage to you. You can likewise capitalize outwardly powers that are around you to assist with getting you roused. You can involve your loved ones as inspiration to make all the difference for you and to assist you with getting t o where you need to be throughout everyday life.

Ponder the drawn out things that you believe you should do and pursue your fantasies. Assuming you have objectives set for yourself later on in the distance, you will see that you can make a solid effort to take care of business. You can utilize your professional inspiration for getting to where you need to be throughout everyday life and in your desired vocation to accomplish. You can have the profession that you have for a long time needed regardless of whether you believe that you it is inconceivable at this moment. There is dependably time to get it going and you should simply have vocation inspiration and assurant

Give yourself discipline. You need to make yourself buckle down for things that you truly need throughout everyday life. There isn't anything in life that is truly worth anything in the event that you don't work for it. Getting a complementary lift won't show you anything inspiration and where you should accompany your very own objectives and joy throughout everyday life. Finish the inspiration strategies that you have learned and you will get to where you need to be and warm hearted about what you have accomplished enroute.